DISCOVE
A COMPREH

BY
WILLIAM JONES
2023

Discovering Albania: A Comprehensive Travel Guide by William Jones
This book edition was created and published by Mamba Press
©MambaPress 2023. All Rights Reserved.

Contents

Preface: Embracing Albania's Warm Embrace
   Introduction: Albania Unveiled
   Chapter 1: Tirana - The Capital City
   Chapter 2: Exploring Ancient Ruins - Butrint and Apollonia
   Chapter 3: The Riviera - Sun, Sand, and Sea
   Chapter 4: Gjirokastër - The City of a Thousand Steps
   Chapter 5: Lush Landscapes of Theth and Valbona
   Chapter 6: Culinary Delights - Albanian Flavors
   Chapter 7: Festivals and Traditions
   Chapter 8: Outdoor Adventures - From Peaks to Beaches
   Chapter 9: Beyond Borders - Exploring Kosovo and Montenegro
   Chapter 10: Sustainable Travel in Albania
   Conclusion: A Tapestry of Memories - Farewell to Albania
   Appendix A: Resources and Useful Information
   Appendix B: Checklist for Long-Term Success

Preface
Embracing Albania's Warm Embrace

Welcome, fellow traveler, to a journey through the hidden heart of the Balkans – Albania. As you embark on this adventure, let the pages of this guide be your compass, guiding you through a land where time seems to slow, history whispers through ancient stones, and the embrace of warm hospitality awaits at every turn.

Albania, often overlooked on the well-trodden paths of European exploration, is a revelation waiting to be uncovered. It is a country where the past meets the present, where echoes of empires resonate in the architecture, and where the landscapes are as diverse as the people who call this land home.

You're about to traverse a country that has emerged from the shadows of a complicated past, eager to share its tales of resilience and renewal. Albania's allure lies not only in its breathtaking landscapes but also in the generosity of its people, the richness of its culture, and the authenticity that permeates every experience.

As you turn these pages, imagine yourself strolling through the vibrant streets of Tirana, the capital that has shed its communist cloak to reveal a city pulsating with life. Sidewalk cafes beckon with the aroma of strong coffee, and the colorful facades of buildings seem to reflect the nation's newfound vibrancy.

But our journey doesn't stop in the capital. Albania's soul resides in its ancient ruins, where the stones of Butrint and Apollonia tell stories of civilizations long past. Feel the weight of history as you wander through amphitheaters and temples, marveling at the architectural wonders that have withstood the tests of time.

Picture yourself winding along the Albanian Riviera, where the Adriatic and Ionian Seas caress pristine beaches. This is where the Mediterranean sun meets the warmth of Albanian hospitality, where coastal villages invite you to savor the slow pace of life and the taste of fresh seafood.

And then there's Gjirokastër, the city of a thousand steps, where Ottoman architecture graces the cobblestone streets. As you explore the narrow alleys and visit the imposing castle, you'll find yourself transported to a bygone era, where the past is not a distant memory but a living, breathing part of the present.

Venture into the Albanian Alps, where Theth and Valbona Valley National Parks offer a rugged escape into nature. Imagine hiking through landscapes that seem untouched by time, encountering traditional stone houses, and forging connections with locals whose warmth mirrors the sun-drenched valleys.

Our journey also leads us to the heart of Albanian culture, where culinary delights await. From the robust flavors of fërgesë to the sweetness of baklava, every bite is a celebration of tradition and taste. Join in local festivals, immerse yourself in the rhythms of traditional music, and dance under the starlit skies – for in Albania, every celebration is an invitation to become part of the community.

Albania is not just a destination; it's an odyssey into the unknown, a tapestry woven with threads of history, culture, and natural beauty. Beyond borders, our exploration extends into neighboring Kosovo and Montenegro, where connections between these Balkan nations come to life.

As you navigate this guide, consider the impact of your travels on the environment and local communities. Embrace sustainable practices, contribute positively to the preservation of Albania's treasures, and leave behind only footprints – leaving the beauty of this land intact for future generations of wanderers.

As you turn the final page, let the spirit of Albania linger in your memories. May your adventures be as enchanting as the stories you've uncovered, the landscapes you've traversed, and the friendships you've forged.

Albania awaits, dear traveler, with open arms and a story to share. Bon voyage!

Introduction
Albania Unveiled

Greetings, intrepid traveler, and welcome to the captivating journey that is Albania. Nestled in the heart of the Balkans, this unassuming gem has long remained in the shadows of its European counterparts, waiting patiently for curious souls like yours to uncover its secrets.

As you prepare to step onto the Albanian soil, it's essential to shed preconceived notions and open your mind to a destination that defies expectations. Albania, with its rich tapestry of history, cultural influences, and natural wonders, invites you to embark on an adventure that transcends the ordinary.

Let's begin our odyssey by peeling back the layers of time. Albania's history is a mosaic of civilizations that have left their indelible mark on the landscape. Imagine ancient Illyrians treading these lands, followed by the Romans, Byzantines, and Ottomans. The echoes of their stories reverberate through the cobblestone streets, the ancient amphitheaters, and the formidable castles that dot the horizon.

Albania's story is not one of smooth transitions; it is a narrative of resilience and rebirth. In the latter half of the 20th century, this small nation experienced the grip of communism, isolating it from the world for decades. The scars of that era are still visible in the concrete bunkers that dot the countryside, a stark reminder of a time when Albania stood as one of the world's most closed societies.

However, as the winds of change swept through Eastern Europe in the early 1990s, Albania emerged from its cocoon, shedding the ideological shackles that bound it. The capital, Tirana, once gray and somber, burst into color as its people embraced newfound freedoms. Today, the vibrant energy of Tirana is a testament to the resilience of a nation that has faced adversity and emerged stronger.

As you walk the streets of Tirana, let the kaleidoscope of colors be a metaphor for Albania's transformation. In the bustling Blloku district, where once only the privileged few could tread, today's cafes, boutiques, and lively street markets bear witness to the country's rebirth. The Pyramid, a former museum honoring the dictator Enver Hoxha, stands as a stark contrast to the modernity that surrounds it, embodying the paradoxical nature of Albania's journey.

Yet, Albania's allure extends beyond its capital. The ancient ruins of Butrint, a UNESCO World Heritage Site, beckon you to a time when this coastal city was a crossroads of civilizations. Imagine wandering through the remnants of a Roman forum, a Byzantine basilica, and a Venetian tower, each layer of history unfolding beneath your footsteps.

But Albania is not just a tapestry of ancient stones; it is a nation defined by its landscapes. The Albanian Riviera, stretching along the Ionian Sea, is a testament to the country's natural beauty. Picture yourself on the beaches of Dhërmi, where turquoise waters lap against golden shores, or in the secluded bays of Ksamil, where time seems to stand still.

As you traverse the Albanian Alps, the rugged landscapes of Theth and Valbona Valley National Parks unfold before you. These pristine wildernesses, with their dramatic peaks, crystal-clear rivers, and traditional stone villages, offer a glimpse into a world untouched by the rush of modernity.

Now, let's talk about the heart and soul of Albania – its people. Albanians are renowned for their hospitality, a trait deeply embedded in their cultural fabric. Prepare to be welcomed with open arms, whether you're sipping strong Turkish coffee in a local kafeneja or sharing stories with villagers in the mountainous north.

And what's a journey without indulging in the flavors of the land? Albanian cuisine is a symphony of tastes, from the hearty fërgesë, a traditional dish with peppers, tomatoes, and feta, to the sweet notes of baklava. Don't just taste the food; let it be a conduit to the stories and traditions passed down through generations.

As we venture into the chapters that follow, we'll explore the hidden corners of Gjirokastër, the city of a thousand steps, where Ottoman architecture whispers tales of centuries gone by. We'll traverse the landscapes of Theth and Valbona, uncover the rhythm of local festivals, and delve into the cultural connections that bind Albania with its neighbors.

Beyond the borders of this small nation, our exploration will extend into Kosovo and Montenegro, unraveling the threads that weave these Balkan nations together. From the cultural similarities to the distinct identities, you'll witness the interconnectedness of a region shaped by its history and geography.

Before we set forth on this expedition, let's pause and acknowledge the responsibility that comes with exploring new lands. As conscientious travelers, we must strive to leave only footprints and cherish the delicate balance between tourism and preservation. Albania's natural wonders and cultural heritage are not just for us to enjoy but are entrusted to us for safekeeping.

So, as you embark on this adventure through the pages of this guide, let your imagination soar, your senses awaken, and your heart open to the warm embrace of Albania. The journey ahead is one of discovery, transformation, and, above all, an invitation to be a part of a story that continues to unfold. Albania awaits – let the unveiling begin.

Chapter 1
Tirana - The Capital City

Tirana, the heartbeat of Albania, pulses with an energy that is both palpable and infectious. As you step into the capital city, prepare to be immersed in a kaleidoscope of colors, sounds, and flavors that reflect the nation's journey from a closed-off communist state to a vibrant, modern European capital.

The cityscape is a vibrant canvas, a testament to Tirana's evolution from a muted past to a present that is anything but subdued. The once-gray buildings, remnants of a bygone era, have undergone a metamorphosis, adorned in hues that seem to defy the city's history. As you stroll through the streets, the eclectic blend of architecture tells the tale of Tirana's resilience and transformation.

Begin your exploration in Skanderbeg Square, the heart of the city, where a statue of the national hero, Gjergj Kastrioti Skanderbeg, stands proudly. This is not merely a square; it is a bustling arena where locals gather, and history unfolds. Admire the Ethem Bey Mosque, its elegant minaret juxtaposed against a backdrop of modernity, a visual representation of the city's harmonious blend of the old and the new.

From Skanderbeg Square, the journey through Tirana's past and present continues to the National Historical Museum. Step inside to explore the exhibits that chronicle Albania's complex history, from Illyrian times to the struggles of World War II and the communist era. The museum is not just a repository of artifacts but a time capsule that invites you to unravel the layers of a nation's identity.

Tirana's vibrancy is perhaps most evident in the transformation of the once-forbidden district of Blloku. This area, once exclusive to party elites, has emerged as a symbol of the city's liberation. Today, its streets are lined with trendy cafes, boutiques, and a thriving nightlife that captivates both locals and visitors alike. Take a seat in one of the cafes, order a strong cup of Albanian coffee, and let the rhythm of the city seep into your soul.

Wandering through Blloku, you'll encounter the House of Leaves, a building with a haunting past. Originally constructed as the headquarters of the Sigurimi, the communist-era secret police, it now houses a museum that peels back the layers of surveillance and paranoia that shrouded Albania during that time. It's a chilling reminder of the not-so-distant past and the resilience of a nation that has emerged from the shadows.

For a panoramic view of the city and the surrounding mountains, make your way to the Dajti Express cable car. As you ascend, Tirana unfolds beneath you like a patchwork quilt, revealing the juxtaposition of modern architecture, communist-era blocks, and Ottoman influences. At the summit, take a moment to breathe in the crisp mountain air and appreciate the landscape that cradles the city.

As the sun sets over Tirana, the city undergoes yet another transformation. The Pyramid, a striking architectural relic of the communist era, stands illuminated against the night sky. Originally intended as a museum honoring Enver Hoxha, it has weathered controversy and transformation to become a symbol of Tirana's unyielding spirit.

Evenings in Tirana are a celebration of life, and nowhere is this more evident than in the trendy district of Blloku. The area comes alive with laughter, music, and the clinking of glasses as locals and visitors alike gather in bars and clubs. Join the festivities, savor the local raki, and let the rhythm of Tirana's nightlife carry you into the early hours.

But Tirana's allure is not confined to its urban landscape. The city is a gateway to the beauty of the surrounding countryside, and a short drive takes you to the serene shores of Lake Tirana. Here, you can escape the urban bustle, stroll along the lakeside promenade, and enjoy a tranquil boat ride with the city's skyline in the distance.

Tirana is not just a city; it is an evolving narrative, a living testament to Albania's journey through time. As you walk its streets, engage with its people, and absorb its history, you'll find that Tirana is more than the sum of its parts – it's a reflection of a nation that has overcome challenges, embraced change, and welcomed the world with open arms.

So, fellow traveler, let Tirana's warmth, vibrancy, and resilience captivate your senses. This is a city that invites you to not just observe but to participate in its ongoing story. As you bid farewell to Skanderbeg Square, the vibrant cafes of Blloku, and the panoramic views from Dajti Mountain, carry with you the essence of Tirana – a city that continues to reinvent itself while staying true to its roots.

Chapter 2
Exploring Ancient Ruins - Butrint and Apollonia

Embark on a journey through time as we venture into the heart of Albania's ancient past. Butrint and Apollonia, two archaeological marvels, beckon with tales of bygone civilizations, whispering through the stones and columns that have weathered centuries. As we explore these ancient ruins, prepare to be transported to a world where history unfolds in every step, and the echoes of the past resonate through the air.

Our first stop is Butrint, a UNESCO World Heritage Site that stands as a testament to the confluence of cultures that have shaped this land. Nestled on the shores of the Vivari Channel, Butrint unfolds like an open-air museum, revealing layers of history that span from the Greeks to the Romans, Byzantines, Venetians, and Ottomans.

The entrance to Butrint is marked by the Lion's Gate, an imposing structure that welcomes you into a world frozen in time. As you pass through this ancient portal, the city unfolds, each step revealing remnants of civilizations that once thrived on this peninsula. The theater, with its well-preserved acoustics, transports you to an era when performances echoed against the backdrop of the Adriatic Sea.

Wander through the Roman forum, where the ruins of temples and public buildings stand as silent witnesses to the city's former glory. Pause at the Baptistery, a masterpiece of early Christian art, its mosaic floor depicting scenes of fish and sea creatures, a nod to Butrint's maritime heritage.

The highlight of Butrint, however, is the Venetian castle that crowns the acropolis. As you ascend to its heights, panoramic views of the Vivari Channel and the surrounding landscape unfold. It's a vista that transcends time, inviting you to reflect on the strategic importance of Butrint throughout the ages.

Butrint is not merely a collection of stones; it is a narrative of resilience and adaptation. The city, once a flourishing trade hub, weathered the storms of time and invasions, leaving behind a mosaic of cultural influences that paint a vivid picture of its past. Explore the remains of the Basilica, the Roman House, and the Great Fort, each offering a glimpse into the complex tapestry of Butrint's history.

Leaving the whispers of Butrint behind, our journey continues to Apollonia, another archaeological gem that unfolds amid the rolling hills of central Albania. As you approach the site, the imposing columns of the Bouleuterion, an ancient meeting place, stand as sentinels, welcoming you to a city that was once dedicated to the Greek god Apollo.

Apollonia, founded in the 6th century BCE, served as a center of learning and culture. Imagine walking through the same colonnades where scholars and philosophers once strolled, engaging in intellectual pursuits that left an indelible mark on the ancient world. The Odeon, a small theater, whispers of performances and gatherings that celebrated the arts and humanities.

Stroll through the monumental entrance of the city, the Propylaea, and feel the weight of history as you stand beneath its towering arch. The Agora, a bustling marketplace in its heyday, invites you to envision the daily lives of ancient Apollonians as they engaged in commerce and communal activities.

As you explore the Temples of Artemis and Zeus, their ruins a testament to the religious fervor that once permeated this city, the air becomes charged with a sense of awe. The sprawling complex of the Monastery of St. Mary, nestled within the archaeological site, adds another layer to Apollonia's narrative, showcasing the city's evolution through the ages.

What sets Apollonia apart is its amphitheater, a marvel of ancient engineering carved into the hillside. Take a seat in the grandstands, and let your imagination transport you to a time when the amphitheater echoed with the cheers of spectators, the clash of gladiatorial combat, and the resonance of theatrical performances.

As you stand on the acropolis of Apollonia, the views extend over the lush landscape that surrounds the city. The Aous River meanders in the distance, a tranquil companion to the ancient stones that have weathered centuries of change. It's a moment of reflection, a chance to appreciate the significance of Apollonia as a crossroads of civilizations and a testament to the endurance of human endeavor.

The beauty of exploring ancient ruins lies not just in the stones and structures but in the stories they tell. Butrint and Apollonia, each with its unique character, offer a glimpse into the ebb and flow of history, where cultures collided, adapted, and left their imprint on the land. These sites are not remnants of a distant past; they are living testaments to the resilience of the human spirit.

As you bid farewell to Butrint and Apollonia, let the echoes of ancient civilizations linger in your thoughts. The stones beneath your feet have borne witness to triumphs and tribulations, to the rise and fall of empires. Carry with you the stories of Butrint's maritime legacy and Apollonia's intellectual prowess as you continue your journey through Albania – a land where the past is not forgotten but celebrated in every ruin, every column, and every stone.

Chapter 3
The Riviera - Sun, Sand, and Sea

Prepare to surrender to the allure of the Albanian Riviera, where the azure waters of the Ionian and Adriatic Seas caress pristine beaches, and charming coastal villages beckon with the promise of a sun-soaked escape. As we embark on this journey along the coastline, let the rhythm of the waves and the warmth of the Mediterranean sun guide us through a landscape that seamlessly blends natural beauty with cultural richness.

Our odyssey begins in Dhërmi, a coastal gem nestled between the Adriatic and the imposing Llogara Pass. As you approach the village, the landscape transforms into a breathtaking panorama of rolling hills, olive groves, and the turquoise expanse of the Ionian Sea. Dhërmi is a haven for those seeking tranquility and seclusion, its beaches framed by rugged cliffs and dotted with quaint seafood restaurants serving up the catch of the day.

Dhërmi's allure lies not only in its natural beauty but also in its authenticity. Take a leisurely stroll through the village, where stone houses adorned with vibrant bougainvillea line narrow cobblestone streets. The scent of sea salt mingles with the aroma of local delicacies, creating an olfactory symphony that captures the essence of the Albanian Riviera.

For those seeking a more active retreat, the beaches of Dhërmi offer an array of water sports, from kayaking to paddleboarding. The crystal-clear waters invite you to plunge in and discover the underwater wonders that lie beneath the surface. Snorkeling or diving reveals a vibrant marine world, where colorful fish dance among the rocks and ancient amphorae tell tales of maritime history.

Continuing southward, the coastal road unfolds like a ribbon, hugging the cliffs and offering panoramic views of the Ionian Sea. Our next stop is Jale, a hidden cove where time seems to stand still. The beach, with its powdery white sand and translucent waters, is a canvas of tranquility.

Find a secluded spot, lay down your towel, and let the gentle lull of the waves be your soundtrack.

The journey along the Riviera is not just about beaches; it's a pilgrimage to Gjipe, a coastal gem tucked away between towering cliffs. Accessible by boat or a scenic hike, Gjipe is a secluded paradise where the Adriatic Sea meets a river, creating a natural oasis of serenity. The beach, framed by limestone cliffs, is a sanctuary for those seeking solitude and a connection with nature.

As we approach Himara, the coastline unveils a mix of history and natural beauty. The old town of Himara, perched on a hill overlooking the sea, is a living testament to the region's past. Explore the narrow alleys, visit the medieval castle, and immerse yourself in a landscape where ancient stones tell stories of empires and maritime adventures.

The journey through the Albanian Riviera reaches its zenith in the town of Ksamil, a coastal jewel where the Ionian Islands beckon on the horizon. Ksamil is renowned for its pristine beaches, each with its own charm and character. Sink your toes into the soft sand, take a dip in the clear waters, and feel the warmth of the sun on your skin.

Ksamil is not just a beach destination; it's a gateway to the surreal beauty of the nearby islands. Hire a boat and set sail to the Ksamil Islands, where secluded beaches and hidden caves await exploration. The islands, scattered like emeralds in the sea, are a testament to the untouched natural beauty that defines this corner of the Mediterranean.

The charm of the Albanian Riviera extends beyond the beaches to the vibrant coastal town of Saranda. As you approach Saranda, the city unfolds like a mosaic of modernity and tradition. The waterfront promenade, adorned with palm trees and cafes, invites you to savor a leisurely stroll as the sun dips below the horizon, casting hues of orange and pink over the sea.

Saranda is not only a hub of activity but also a gateway to some of Albania's most intriguing archaeological sites. A short boat ride takes you to the ancient city of Butrint, where the ruins tell stories of civilizations that once thrived in this coastal enclave. Explore the amphitheater, the Roman baths, and the baptistery, each offering a glimpse into Butrint's rich history.

For a change of pace, head to the Lëkurësi Castle, perched on a hill overlooking Saranda. The panoramic views from the castle extend across the town, the sea, and the distant islands. It's an ideal spot to watch the sunset, with the lights of Saranda twinkling below as the day transforms into night.

The Albanian Riviera is not merely a destination; it's an experience that transcends the ordinary. Whether you seek relaxation on sun-drenched beaches, adventure in hidden coves, or a taste of history in coastal towns, the Riviera unfolds as a tapestry of diversity and charm.

As we conclude our exploration of the Riviera, let the sound of the waves, the warmth of the sun, and the hospitality of the coastal villages linger in your memories. The journey along this stretch of paradise is a celebration of life, a dance between land and sea that invites you to lose yourself in the beauty of the Albanian Riviera – a destination where sun, sand, and sea converge to create an unforgettable symphony of experiences.

Chapter 4
Gjirokastër - The City of a Thousand Steps

Welcome to Gjirokastër, a city where time seems to have paused, and history unfolds in the cobblestone streets, the Ottoman-style houses, and the imposing castle that looms over the landscape. Known as the "City of a Thousand Steps," Gjirokastër is a living museum, a captivating journey through the centuries where the echoes of the past resonate with every footfall.

As you approach Gjirokastër, nestled in the picturesque Drino Valley, the city's silhouette emerges on the horizon. The towering minarets and the distinctive stone roofs of the Ottoman houses create a scene that transports you to another era. Gjirokastër, a UNESCO World Heritage Site, is not just a city; it's an architectural marvel, a testament to the diverse cultural influences that have shaped Albania over the centuries.

Begin your exploration in the heart of the old town, where the bazaar comes alive with the sights and sounds of daily life. Picture yourself wandering through narrow alleys flanked by Ottoman-era houses, their whitewashed walls adorned with wooden balconies and colorful flowers. The air is infused with the scent of traditional pastries, freshly brewed coffee, and the occasional waft of spices from local markets.

One of Gjirokastër's most iconic landmarks is the Zekate House, an Ottoman-era mansion that provides a glimpse into the opulence of times gone by. As you step into its well-preserved rooms, adorned with intricate woodwork and adorned ceilings, you'll find yourself transported to an era when Gjirokastër was a bustling center of commerce and culture.

The charm of Gjirokastër lies not just in its architectural treasures but in the warmth of its people. Engage with locals in the bazaar, strike up a conversation with shopkeepers, and let the stories of the city unfold through the voices of those who call it home. Gjirokastër is not a city frozen in time; it's a vibrant community that carries its history with pride while embracing the present.

A defining feature of Gjirokastër is its castle, a fortress that has stood sentinel over the city for centuries. As you ascend the cobblestone path leading to the castle gates, the panoramic views of Gjirokastër and the surrounding mountains unfold before you. The castle, with its imposing walls and towers, is not merely a historic site but a vantage point that offers a profound understanding of the city's strategic importance.

Inside the castle, the Ethnographic Museum awaits, housed in a renovated Ottoman building. The museum provides a window into the daily lives of Gjirokastër's residents over the centuries, showcasing traditional costumes, tools, and artifacts that speak to the city's rich cultural heritage. It's a journey through time that complements the immersive experience of exploring the castle's medieval walls.

Gjirokastër's castle also holds the Gjirokastër Arms Museum, a collection of weaponry and military artifacts that reflects the city's role in various historical conflicts. As you navigate the exhibits, you'll gain insights into Gjirokastër's resilience and the strategic challenges it faced throughout its storied history.

The charm of Gjirokastër extends beyond its historical sites to its vibrant cultural scene. The city has been a cradle of intellectual and artistic activity, and the birthplace of renowned Albanian writer Ismail Kadare. Immerse yourself in the literary ambiance of the city, where bookshops line the streets, and the echoes of Kadare's words seem to linger in the air.

Gjirokastër's commitment to preserving its cultural heritage is evident in events like the National Folklore Festival, where traditional music, dance, and crafts take center stage. If your visit coincides with this celebration, you'll have the opportunity to witness the dynamic expressions of Gjirokastër's living traditions.

No visit to Gjirokastër is complete without exploring the Bazaar of Gjirokastër, a vibrant marketplace where the spirit of the city comes alive. From handmade crafts to local delicacies, the bazaar is a treasure trove of souvenirs and experiences. Engage with artisans, sample regional products, and take a piece of Gjirokastër's charm home with you.

As the sun sets over the city, Gjirokastër undergoes a metamorphosis. The warm glow of streetlights illuminates the cobblestone streets, casting shadows on the Ottoman houses that seem to whisper tales of the past. The castle, now perched against the night sky, becomes a silhouette of history, a guardian watching over Gjirokastër as it sleeps.

Gjirokastër is not just a city to be observed; it's a destination to be felt, experienced, and embraced. It's a place where history converges with contemporary life, where the rhythm of the present harmonizes with the echoes of the past. The "City of a Thousand Steps" invites you to take each step deliberately, savoring the layers of history, culture, and authenticity that unfold with every stride.

As you bid farewell to Gjirokastër, let the memories of its winding streets, its Ottoman houses, and its castle linger in your heart. The "City of a Thousand Steps" is not just a stop on your journey through Albania; it's a chapter in your travel story, a testament to the enduring beauty and charm of a city that invites you to step back in time while embracing the present.

Chapter 5
Lush Landscapes of Theth and Valbona

Venture into the rugged beauty of northern Albania, where the landscapes of Theth and Valbona Valley unfold like pages from a storybook. Far removed from the bustling cities and coastal retreats, these pristine wildernesses invite you to embark on a journey through nature's tapestry, where majestic mountains, crystal-clear rivers, and traditional stone villages create a haven for those seeking an immersive escape into the heart of Albania.

Our odyssey begins in Theth, a remote village nestled within the Accursed Mountains. As you wind through the scenic journey from Shkodra, the landscape gradually transforms into a rugged terrain of towering peaks and lush valleys. Theth, surrounded by snow-capped mountains, is a testament to the untouched beauty that defines northern Albania.

Theth welcomes you with open arms, its stone houses and distinctive tower-shaped kulla buildings blending seamlessly with the natural surroundings. The village exudes an air of tranquility, a place where time seems to move at its own pace. Stroll through the cobblestone streets, where the murmur of the Shala River serves as a melodic backdrop to the whispers of the wind in the trees.

The heart of Theth lies in its iconic church and the Lock-in Tower, a centuries-old structure that served as a refuge during times of blood feuds. As you explore these historic landmarks, you'll find that Theth is not merely a destination; it's a living museum where the stories of the past echo through the walls and the surrounding mountains.

From Theth, the trail leads to the Grunas Waterfall, a hidden gem enveloped by lush greenery. The hike is a journey through nature's wonders, where the scent of pine trees and the sound of rustling leaves accompany you along the path. As the waterfall comes into view, cascading down the rocks in a symphony of nature, you'll understand why Theth is a magnet for hikers and nature enthusiasts.

For those seeking a more challenging trek, the path to the Blue Eye awaits. This natural spring, with its vibrant blue hues, is a tranquil oasis surrounded by dense forests. The journey is as rewarding as the destination, with the opportunity to immerse yourself in the untamed landscapes that characterize Theth.

As the day draws to a close, Theth unveils its nocturnal charm. Away from the glow of city lights, the village is a canvas of stars, and the crisp mountain air invites you to contemplate the vastness of the universe. In Theth, the night sky becomes a spectacle, a stark contrast to the urban landscapes left behind.

Our journey continues eastward, traversing the Valbona Pass that connects Theth to Valbona Valley. The road offers panoramic views of the Albanian Alps, where the peaks seem to touch the heavens. Valbona Valley, a secluded haven cradled by the mountains, welcomes you with open arms, its landscapes a poetic interplay of rugged terrain and alpine meadows.

Valbona is a destination that beckons to those seeking refuge in nature's embrace. The valley is dotted with traditional wooden houses, their colorful shutters standing out against the backdrop of greenery. The Valbona River, with its crystal-clear waters, winds its way through the valley, inviting you to pause and immerse yourself in the soothing sounds of nature.

Embark on a trek through the Valbona Pass, where the panoramic views stretch across the valley and the surrounding peaks. The journey is a meditative experience, where the rhythm of your footsteps harmonizes with the symphony of nature. As you ascend, the air becomes crisper, and the landscapes more dramatic, unveiling the raw beauty that defines the Albanian Alps.

At the heart of Valbona, the village and its people offer a glimpse into a way of life deeply rooted in the rhythms of the seasons. Engage with locals, share stories over a cup of mountain tea, and let the warmth of their hospitality envelop you. In Valbona, the sense of community is palpable, and visitors become temporary custodians of the valley's tranquility.

For the avid hiker, the trek to Rosi Peak is a thrilling adventure that rewards with panoramic views of the surrounding peaks and valleys. As you stand at the summit, the Albanian Alps unfold beneath you, a landscape of rugged beauty that stretches into the horizon. It's a moment of triumph, where the challenges of the journey become insignificantly small in comparison to the grandeur of nature.

A journey through Valbona Valley is not just about reaching summits; it's a celebration of the journey itself. The trail from Valbona to Theth, often referred to as the Peaks of the Balkans Trail, is a multi-day trek that traverses the Albanian Alps, connecting remote villages and showcasing the diversity of the region's landscapes.

As the sun sets over Valbona Valley, the landscapes take on a golden hue, casting a warm glow over the mountains and meadows. The night sky, free from the ambient glow of urban lights, becomes a canvas of stars, inviting contemplation and reflection. In Valbona, each night is a quiet symphony, where the only sounds are those of nature and the occasional rustle of leaves in the breeze.

As you bid farewell to Theth and Valbona, let the echoes of nature's symphony linger in your memories. These landscapes, with their untamed beauty and secluded charm, are not merely destinations but gateways to experiences that transcend the ordinary. In Theth and Valbona, the mountains, rivers, and villages become chapters in a story that invites you to reconnect with nature, rediscover simplicity, and immerse yourself in the timeless allure of Albania's northern wilderness.

Chapter 6
Culinary Delights - Albanian Flavors

Prepare your taste buds for a journey through the rich and diverse tapestry of Albanian cuisine. Beyond the historical sites and breathtaking landscapes, Albania reveals itself as a culinary gem, offering a feast of flavors deeply rooted in tradition, shaped by history, and influenced by the country's diverse cultural heritage. As you embark on this gastronomic adventure, let the warmth of Albanian hospitality and the aromas of local markets be your guides.

Begin your culinary exploration with a sip of Turkish coffee, a ubiquitous presence in Albanian culture. Served strong and unfiltered, this aromatic elixir is more than just a beverage; it's a ritual that invites conversation, connection, and a moment of reflection. As you enjoy your coffee in a local kafeneja, surrounded by the hum of conversation and the scent of freshly brewed beans, you'll discover that this is where the essence of Albanian hospitality unfolds.

Albanian breakfasts are hearty affairs, often featuring byrek, a savory pastry that comes in various forms. Whether filled with cheese, spinach, or minced meat, byrek is a staple of Albanian households and bakeries. The delicate layers of dough enveloping a flavorful filling create a symphony of textures, making it a perfect start to the day.

Journey into the heart of Albanian markets, where the vibrant colors of fresh produce and the lively banter of vendors create a sensory spectacle. Here, you'll find an array of fruits, vegetables, and herbs, each bursting with flavor and vibrancy. Engage with local sellers, sample seasonal delights, and let the market be your introduction to the bounty of Albanian agriculture.

No exploration of Albanian cuisine is complete without indulging in the country's rich dairy offerings. Feta cheese, a crumbly and tangy delight, is a ubiquitous presence in Albanian kitchens. Whether enjoyed on its own, sprinkled over salads, or folded into pastries, Albanian feta adds a distinctive touch to many dishes.

As you venture further into Albania, discover the delights of tave kosi, a traditional baked lamb and yogurt dish. The tender lamb, slow-cooked to perfection, is enveloped in a velvety blanket of yogurt and eggs. Tave kosi is a celebration of simplicity and flavors, capturing the essence of Albanian home cooking.

For seafood enthusiasts, the coastal regions of Albania beckon with a bounty from the Adriatic and Ionian Seas. Try the delectable grilë, grilled sea bass or sea bream, seasoned with local herbs and olive oil. The freshness of the catch, combined with the simplicity of preparation, allows the natural flavors to shine through.

Albania's culinary landscape is also marked by the legacy of Ottoman influence, evident in dishes like qofte, seasoned meatballs that are a favorite street food. Served in a bun or with a side of vegetables, qofte is a savory delight that showcases the blend of flavors that define Albanian cuisine.

Meat lovers will find joy in dishes like fërgesë, a hearty stew featuring peppers, tomatoes, and feta cheese, combined with meat, often veal or lamb. The slow-cooked medley of flavors creates a comforting dish that reflects the heartiness of Albanian mountain cuisine.

One of the crown jewels of Albanian sweets is baklava, a rich and indulgent pastry that traces its roots back to the Ottoman Empire. Layers of filo dough, butter, and finely chopped nuts are baked to perfection, then soaked in a honey or sugar syrup. The result is a sweet symphony of textures and flavors that captivates the senses.

To wash down these delectable treats, explore the world of rakia, a traditional Albanian brandy made from fruits like grapes or plums. Rakia is not just a drink; it's a cultural experience, often shared during celebrations, toasts, and moments of camaraderie. Let the robust spirit of rakia become a companion to your culinary journey through Albania.

Albanian hospitality is perhaps most evident in the tradition of fërgesa e Tiranës, a hearty dish named after the capital city, Tirana. Comprising green and red peppers, tomatoes, onions, and feta cheese, fërgesa e Tiranës captures the essence of Albanian flavors. Served with a side of crusty bread, this dish exemplifies the country's commitment to fresh, locally sourced ingredients.

As you dine in Albanian restaurants, you'll discover the art of slow food, a philosophy that places emphasis on the quality of ingredients and the pleasure of shared meals. Përshëndetje, the Albanian equivalent of "cheers," is more than just a toast; it's an expression of camaraderie, a shared moment of joy around the dining table.

Albanian culinary experiences extend beyond urban centers to the charming agrotourism farms scattered throughout the countryside. Here, you can indulge in farm-to-table delights, savoring dishes prepared with ingredients harvested from the surrounding fields. Engage with local hosts, learn about traditional cooking methods, and immerse yourself in the authenticity of Albanian rural life.

As you traverse Albania, from the northern mountains to the southern riviera, each region unveils its unique culinary treasures. In Korçë, savor the local specialty lakror, a savory pastry filled with seasonal vegetables or meat. In Gjirokastër, delight in tave dheu, a baked dish featuring lamb, rice, and yogurt.

The Albanian dining experience is not just about the food; it's about the connection between people, the celebration of flavors, and the exploration of a culinary heritage that spans centuries. Engage with locals, ask for recommendations, and let the dining table become a stage for cultural exchange and discovery.

As your culinary journey through Albania draws to a close, let the flavors linger on your palate and the memories of shared meals become a cherished part of your travel narrative. Albania's culinary landscape is a symphony of tastes, an invitation to savor the richness of tradition, and an exploration of a nation's history through its diverse and delectable dishes. So, fellow traveler, raise your glass, savor each bite, and let the culinary delights of Albania become a vibrant chapter in your global gastronomic adventure.

Chapter 7
Festivals and Traditions

Step into the vibrant tapestry of Albanian culture, where traditions are woven into the fabric of daily life, and festivals become living expressions of history, community, and joy. As you traverse this land of rich heritage, you'll find that Albanian celebrations are not just events; they are gateways to the soul of the nation, offering a glimpse into the rhythm of life, the warmth of hospitality, and the enduring spirit that defines the Albanian people.

Begin your journey through the tapestry of Albanian traditions by immersing yourself in the lively atmosphere of the Tirana International Film Festival. Held annually in the capital city, this cinematic celebration brings together filmmakers, artists, and cinephiles from around the world. The festival not only showcases the best of Albanian cinema but also fosters cultural exchange, creating a space where stories are told, perspectives are shared, and the magic of the silver screen unites diverse voices.

As you explore the bustling streets of Tirana during the film festival, you'll feel the city's creative pulse, from the eclectic art scene to the vibrant street murals that adorn the urban landscape. Tirana, a city that has undergone a remarkable transformation in recent years, stands as a testament to Albania's embrace of contemporary culture while honoring its historical roots.

Venture into the heart of the Albanian Riviera during the Dhermi Fire Festival, an annual event that lights up the night sky with a spectacular display of flames and fireworks. This unique celebration, rooted in ancient pagan traditions, marks the arrival of spring and the triumph of light over darkness. As the fires blaze on the beaches of Dhermi, locals and visitors alike come together to dance, sing, and revel in the warmth of the flames.

In the town of Gjirokastër, the National Folklore Festival unfolds as a vibrant showcase of Albania's rich cultural heritage. Held every four years, this event brings together folk ensembles, dancers, and musicians from across the country, transforming the city into a living canvas of traditional artistry. Gjirokastër, known as the "City of a Thousand Steps," comes alive with the rhythmic beats of dance, the melodies of folk music, and the colorful costumes that pay homage to Albania's diverse regional traditions.

For those with a penchant for the theatrical, the Gjirokastër National Folklore Festival is an immersive experience that transcends the stage. The performances, deeply rooted in local folklore, tell stories of love, resilience, and the ebb and flow of life in Albania. As you witness the dancers twirl in vibrant costumes and the music reverberates through the air, you'll find yourself transported to a realm where tradition and modernity seamlessly converge.

Albania's festival calendar is also punctuated by religious celebrations that reflect the country's diverse religious landscape. Explore the city of Korçë during the Feast of St. George, a Christian celebration that spills into the streets with processions, music, and joyous gatherings. The colorful traditions of St. George's Feast showcase the coexistence of different religious communities in Albania, where Orthodox Christians, Muslims, and other faiths celebrate side by side.

As you delve into the festivities, you'll discover that Albanian celebrations are not confined to religious or cultural boundaries. They are inclusive, inviting everyone to partake in the communal spirit that defines the nation. The celebrations become a reflection of the unity that emerged from Albania's complex history, where diverse communities found common ground in shared traditions and mutual respect.

Journey to the city of Shkodra during the Virgil Night celebration, an annual event that pays homage to the Roman poet Virgil, believed to have been born in the region. The streets come alive with processions, theatrical performances, and readings of Virgil's poetry, creating a magical atmosphere that transports you back in time. Shkodra, with its rich historical tapestry, becomes a stage where ancient and modern elements intertwine.

For a taste of Albania's ancient Illyrian roots, immerse yourself in the Illyrian Festival in the city of Kukës. This event, held against the backdrop of the stunning Kukës Lake, celebrates the heritage of the Illyrian people, the ancient inhabitants of the region. The festival is a testament to Albania's commitment to preserving its pre-Roman history, offering visitors a chance to engage with archaeologists, historians, and cultural enthusiasts who share a passion for uncovering the secrets of the past.

As you navigate the festivities, take a moment to explore the city of Kukës and its surroundings. The Illyrian Festival becomes an opportunity not only to revel in the festivities but also to connect with the landscapes that have witnessed centuries of history. The ancient ruins, the azure waters of the lake, and the surrounding mountains become silent witnesses to the passage of time and the resilience of the Albanian spirit.

Albania's festival calendar is marked by the diversity of celebrations, from ancient traditions to contemporary expressions of art and culture. The Përmet Carnival, for instance, transforms the town of Përmet into a kaleidoscope of colors, music, and revelry. This lively event, with its vibrant parades and masked participants, is a whimsical celebration that embodies the playful spirit of Albanian culture.

In the city of Berat, the White Night Festival bathes the UNESCO World Heritage Site in a mystical glow. The medieval castle, historic buildings, and ancient streets become a canvas for light installations, creating an enchanting ambiance that draws locals and visitors alike. The White Night Festival is a fusion of tradition and innovation, where the ancient cityscape becomes a contemporary masterpiece.

Albania's festivals are not only about grand celebrations in cities and towns; they also extend to the countryside, where agrotourism farms become stages for authentic experiences. The Harvest Festival, celebrated in various regions across the country, invites travelers to partake in the age-old rituals of grape and olive harvesting. From stomping grapes to pressing olives, you can engage in hands-on activities that connect you with the agricultural traditions that sustain Albanian communities.

As you participate in the Harvest Festival, you'll find that the traditions are not mere spectacles for tourists but living practices that form the backbone of Albanian rural life. The sense of community, the shared labor, and the joy that accompanies the harvest become tangible expressions of a way of life deeply intertwined with the land.

For those seeking a spiritual retreat, Albania offers a unique pilgrimage experience during the annual Bektashi Tekke Pilgrimage. The Bektashi Order, a Sufi Muslim sect with deep roots in Albanian culture, gathers at the Tekke of Baba Ali Tomë in Krujë for a pilgrimage that transcends religious boundaries. Pilgrims, whether Muslim or from other faiths, come together to celebrate unity, tolerance, and the teachings of Baba Ali Tomë.

The Bektashi Tekke Pilgrimage is not just a religious event; it's a cultural phenomenon that highlights Albania's commitment to religious harmony. The pilgrimage becomes a canvas of diversity, where individuals from different backgrounds converge in a spirit of solidarity and mutual respect. It's an opportunity to witness the coexistence of faiths and the role of spirituality in shaping the cultural identity of Albania.

Albania's festival calendar is a reflection of the nation's resilience, creativity, and the enduring spirit of its people. Whether you find yourself immersed in the rhythmic beats of folk music, the vibrant colors of parades, or the serene atmosphere of religious pilgrimages, each festival offers a unique window into the soul of Albania.

As you traverse the country, from the ancient cities to the mountain villages, let the festivals become a living connection to the people and their stories. Engage with locals, participate in the celebrations, and allow the spirit of Albania's festivals to linger in your memories. In the dance of traditions and the music of celebrations, you'll discover that Albania's cultural heritage is not confined to the pages of history; it's a dynamic, living tapestry that invites you to become part of the story.

Chapter 8
Outdoor Adventures - From Peaks to Beaches

Embrace the allure of Albania's outdoor wonders, where rugged landscapes, untamed wilderness, and pristine coastlines beckon adventurers seeking a thrill. Whether you're drawn to the challenge of conquering mountain peaks or yearning for the sun-kissed embrace of the Adriatic Sea, Albania's diverse terrain offers a playground for outdoor enthusiasts, inviting you to embark on unforgettable adventures that span from lofty heights to sandy shores.

Begin your odyssey in the Accursed Mountains, a rugged range that stretches across northern Albania and beckons intrepid explorers with its majestic peaks and pristine valleys. Theth and Valbona, nestled within this mountainous realm, serve as gateways to a trekking paradise. Lace up your hiking boots and traverse trails that lead to hidden waterfalls, alpine lakes, and panoramic vistas that seem to touch the heavens.

The Peaks of the Balkans Trail, a transnational trek that traverses Albania, Kosovo, and Montenegro, takes you deep into the heart of the Accursed Mountains. This multi-day adventure immerses you in the pristine landscapes of Theth and Valbona, where the trails unfold like ancient pathways, connecting remote villages and revealing the untamed beauty of Albania's northern wilderness.

As you ascend the Valbona Pass, the landscapes transform with each step, from lush valleys to rocky ridges that offer unobstructed views of the surrounding peaks. The journey becomes a symphony of nature, where the echoes of your footsteps harmonize with the rustle of leaves, the murmur of rivers, and the occasional call of distant birds. It's an immersive experience that transcends the ordinary, inviting you to embrace the raw beauty of the Accursed Mountains.

For those seeking a more challenging ascent, the trek to Jezerca, the highest peak in the Accursed Mountains, promises a summit experience like no other. The trail to Jezerca navigates through alpine meadows, rocky slopes, and, at higher elevations, patches of snow. As you stand atop Jezerca, the panoramic views extend across the mountain range, revealing a landscape that epitomizes the grandeur of Albania's northern frontier.

The Accursed Mountains are not only a haven for hikers but also a playground for rock climbers. The limestone cliffs of the Theth and Valbona valleys beckon with their vertical challenges, offering routes that cater to both novice climbers and seasoned alpinists. As you ascend the rock faces, the landscapes below transform into a patchwork of greenery, dotted with traditional stone houses and the winding trails you conquered.

Venture further south to the Llogara Pass, a breathtaking mountain pass that connects the Adriatic and Ionian coasts. The Llogara Pass is not merely a road; it's an adventure in itself, with its serpentine twists and turns that lead to an altitude of over 1,000 meters. As you navigate the pass, the vistas unfold before you, revealing the azure waters of the Ionian Sea on one side and the rugged mountains on the other.

The Llogara Pass is a gateway to the Cika and Nemërçka Mountains, where hiking trails meander through forests of pine and fir, leading to hidden springs and panoramic viewpoints. The sense of solitude and tranquility becomes your constant companion, allowing you to disconnect from the demands of the modern world and reconnect with the pristine landscapes that define southern Albania.

For a true mountaineering challenge, set your sights on the Korab Mountain, the highest peak in Albania and the entire Dinaric Alps. The ascent to Korab takes you through beech and pine forests, alpine meadows, and rocky terrain. The reward at the summit is unparalleled, with views that extend across the Macedonian and Kosovo landscapes, revealing the vastness of the Balkan Peninsula.

As you conquer the peaks of the Accursed Mountains, the Llogara Pass, and Korab, let the sense of achievement be accompanied by the realization that Albania's mountains are not merely physical challenges; they are gateways to self-discovery, offering moments of solitude, reflection, and awe-inspiring beauty.

Transition from the mountainous north to the sun-drenched shores of the Albanian Riviera, where a different kind of adventure awaits. The Riviera is not just a destination for sunbathing and relaxation; it's a playground for water enthusiasts, with a myriad of activities that invite you to explore the azure waters of the Ionian and Adriatic Seas.

Dive into the depths of the Ionian Sea, where underwater landscapes teem with marine life and ancient artifacts. The Albanian Riviera, with its crystal-clear waters, offers excellent conditions for snorkeling and scuba diving. Explore hidden caves, underwater rock formations, and encounter a vibrant array of fish that call the Adriatic and Ionian home.

The Riviera is also a haven for water sports enthusiasts. From paddleboarding along the tranquil coves of Dhërmi to kayaking in the azure waters of Ksamil, the coastline becomes your playground. The rhythmic paddling, the gentle lull of the waves, and the sea breeze against your skin create an aquatic symphony that complements the natural beauty of the Riviera.

As you explore the coastal towns of Himara, Jale, and Ksamil, take advantage of the local outfitters offering boat tours to the hidden gems of the Ionian and Adriatic. Sail to Gjipe, a secluded cove framed by towering cliffs, or venture to the Ksamil Islands, where pristine beaches and turquoise waters await exploration. The boat tours become a journey into the secrets of the Riviera, unveiling landscapes that can only be accessed from the sea.

The Riviera's coastal trails, winding along cliffs and beaches, provide a different perspective for hiking enthusiasts. The Llogara Pass, once conquered by road, now reveals its wild side through hiking routes that lead to secluded beaches and panoramic viewpoints. The juxtaposition of mountain and sea creates a dynamic landscape that reflects the diversity of Albania's natural wonders.

Inland from the Riviera lies the mesmerizing Blue Eye, a natural spring with crystal-clear waters that form a mesmerizing shade of blue. The Blue Eye is more than just a scenic wonder; it's an invitation to immerse yourself in the beauty of Albania's freshwater ecosystems. Take a refreshing dip in the cool waters or simply marvel at the natural spectacle that unfolds before you.

Transitioning from the coast to the rivers, Albania's waterways offer a different kind of adventure. The Vjosa River, one of Europe's last wild rivers, invites kayakers and rafters to navigate its rapids and explore the pristine landscapes that line its banks. The Vjosa is not merely a watercourse; it's a living entity that sustains a rich ecosystem and provides a corridor for aquatic adventures.

For those seeking a more relaxed water experience, the Osumi River Canyon offers a tranquil setting for a leisurely paddle. The canyon, with its towering cliffs and lush vegetation, creates a serene backdrop as you navigate the gentle currents. The Osumi River, winding through the heart of southern Albania, is a testament to the country's commitment to preserving its natural wonders.

Albania's outdoor adventures extend beyond the peaks and beaches to the country's national parks, where diverse ecosystems and rare wildlife thrive. The Llogara Pass is the gateway to Llogara Pass National Park, a protected area that encompasses the Cika and Nemërçka Mountains. Hike through ancient beech forests, spot diverse bird species, and revel in the tranquility of nature.

Further inland, explore the wonders of Shebenik-Jabllanicë National Park, where dense forests, alpine meadows, and pristine lakes create a haven for nature lovers. The park, named after its two highest peaks, is a sanctuary for brown bears, wolves, and rare bird species. Hike the trails that wind through this untouched wilderness, and let the sights and sounds of nature become your companions.

As you embark on these outdoor adventures, whether conquering mountain peaks, exploring coastal trails, or paddling through rivers, let the spirit of Albania's diverse landscapes infuse your journey with a sense of wonder and discovery. The mountains, the seas, and the national parks become more than just settings for outdoor activities; they become stages for transformative experiences, moments of connection with nature, and chapters in your personal adventure story.

In Albania, the call of the mountains echoes through the valleys, and the rhythm of the seas accompanies the journey along the coastline. The outdoor wonders are not merely destinations; they are invitations to explore, to challenge yourself, and to savor the untamed beauty that defines this corner of the Balkans. So, fellow adventurer, lace up your boots, unfurl your sails, and let Albania's outdoor wonders become the backdrop for your most unforgettable escapades.

Chapter 9
Beyond Borders - Exploring Kosovo and Montenegro

Embark on an enchanting journey beyond the borders of Albania, where the tapestry of the Balkans unfolds to reveal the hidden gems of Kosovo and Montenegro. Each with its own unique charm, these neighboring countries beckon the intrepid traveler with a promise of rich history, diverse cultures, and landscapes that captivate the soul. Venture into the heart of the Balkans, where every step is a discovery and every border crossed opens a new chapter in your travel narrative.

Begin your cross-border exploration in Kosovo, a land with a complex history that has shaped its unique identity. Prishtina, the capital, pulsates with youthful energy, a reflection of Kosovo's resilience and determination to move forward. Stroll through the vibrant streets adorned with colorful graffiti and murals, and you'll feel the heartbeat of a nation that has emerged from the shadows of the past.

As you explore Prishtina, pause at the Newborn Monument, an ever-changing canvas that captures the spirit of Kosovo's journey to independence. Covered in vibrant graffiti and messages of hope, the monument becomes a living testament to the aspirations and dreams of the people. Engage with locals at the nearby cafés, where the aroma of freshly brewed coffee mingles with the conversations that echo the city's dynamic spirit.

For a deeper dive into Kosovo's history, visit the Kosovo Museum and the Imperial Mosque. The museum houses artifacts that trace the region's ancient past, from Illyrian settlements to Ottoman rule. The Imperial Mosque, a symbol of Prishtina's diverse heritage, invites you to step into a serene space that reflects the legacy of Ottoman architecture.

Travel south to the town of Peja, nestled at the foothills of the Accursed Mountains. Here, the iconic Patriarchate of Peć, a UNESCO World Heritage Site, stands as a testament to the region's medieval past.

The complex of churches, adorned with vibrant frescoes, transports you back in time, offering a glimpse into the cultural richness that flourished in Kosovo centuries ago.

The Rugova Gorge, near Peja, is a natural wonder that beckons with its towering cliffs, lush forests, and the pristine waters of the Lumbardhi River. Hike through the gorge, where the sound of rushing water accompanies your journey, and emerge into the valley to discover the picturesque village of Boge. The rugged beauty of Rugova Gorge is a testament to Kosovo's untamed landscapes, where adventure and serenity coexist.

Journey to the city of Gjakova, where Ottoman-era architecture and cobbled streets create a nostalgic ambiance. The Old Bazaar, a lively market where locals and visitors converge, offers a taste of traditional Kosovar crafts, from handmade textiles to copperware. Gjakova is a haven for those seeking to immerse themselves in Kosovo's living traditions and the warmth of its people.

Crossing into Montenegro, the Bay of Kotor unfolds like a Mediterranean dream, surrounded by mountains that plunge into the Adriatic Sea. The town of Kotor, nestled within the bay, is a UNESCO World Heritage Site that enchants with its medieval charm. Wander through the narrow alleys, where Venetian architecture and ancient walls tell tales of centuries past.

Climb the steps to the fortress atop the hill, and you'll be rewarded with panoramic views of Kotor and the Bay of Kotor. The landscapes, a harmonious blend of sea and mountains, become a canvas that captures the imagination. As the sun sets over the bay, the town below is bathed in a warm glow, creating a magical atmosphere that lingers in your memories.

The coastal town of Budva, with its medieval Old Town and sandy beaches, invites you to bask in the Mediterranean sun. Explore the cobbled streets, where history and modernity coalesce, and discover the remnants of ancient fortifications that once guarded the town. Budva's beaches, kissed by the gentle waves of the Adriatic, offer a tranquil escape for those seeking relaxation by the sea.

Journey into the heart of Montenegro, where the Durmitor National Park unveils a landscape of dramatic beauty. The Tara River Canyon, the second deepest canyon in the world, cuts through the rugged terrain, creating a natural wonder that beckons adventurers. Raft down the Tara River, where the turquoise waters carve through the limestone cliffs, and the sheer magnitude of the canyon becomes your companion.

For those seeking a more serene experience, explore the Black Lake, nestled amidst the Durmitor Mountains. The reflections of the surrounding peaks on the lake's surface create a mirror-like illusion, and the crisp mountain air becomes the soundtrack to your exploration. Durmitor National Park is a sanctuary for hikers, nature enthusiasts, and those yearning for the tranquility of Montenegro's mountain landscapes.

The UNESCO-listed town of Cetinje, once the royal capital of Montenegro, invites you to step back in time. The historic buildings, including the Cetinje Monastery and the Presidential Palace, reflect the nation's rich history and its journey to independence. Wander through the streets, where the sense of nostalgia is palpable, and engage with locals at the charming cafés that line the boulevards.

As you traverse Montenegro, from the coastal towns to the mountainous landscapes, the Bay of Kotor becomes a constant companion. The serpentine road that hugs the bay's contours offers breathtaking views at every turn. Stop at the village of Perast, where the islets of Our Lady of the Rocks and St. George unfold like tales from a maritime fable. Cruise across the bay to these islets, and you'll discover the stories behind the churches and legends that have shaped the bay's cultural tapestry.

The Adriatic town of Bar, with its Ottoman-era Old Town and historic fortress, marks the southern gateway to Montenegro. Explore the ruins of the Old Town, where centuries-old buildings and ancient walls stand as witnesses to the region's turbulent past. The Bar Aqueduct, a testament to Roman engineering, echoes with whispers of bygone eras.

Crossing back into Kosovo, venture to the city of Prizren, where the Bistrica River meanders through the cobbled streets. Prizren, with its Ottoman architecture and vibrant cultural scene, is a testament to the coexistence of different communities in Kosovo. The Sinan Pasha Mosque and the League of Prizren Complex offer glimpses into the city's historical and cultural heritage.

For a panoramic perspective of Kosovo and the surrounding mountains, ascend to the Prizren Fortress. The climb is rewarded with views that stretch across the city and the distant landscapes. The fortress, perched atop the hill, becomes a vantage point from which to contemplate the interconnected histories of Kosovo, Montenegro, and the wider Balkan region.

As you traverse Kosovo and Montenegro, let the cultural diversity, the scenic wonders, and the warmth of the people become threads in the rich tapestry of your journey. Beyond borders, you'll discover that the Balkans are a mosaic of histories, traditions, and landscapes that invite exploration, connection, and a deeper understanding of the region's complexities.

In Kosovo, you'll witness the resilience of a nation that has overcome adversity, and in Montenegro, you'll be captivated by the harmonious blend of sea and mountain. Each step across borders becomes a bridge to new experiences, a tapestry woven with stories of the past and the vibrant energy of the present.

So, fellow traveler, cross the thresholds of Kosovo and Montenegro, let the landscapes unfold before you, and immerse yourself in the cultures that shape this corner of the Balkans. Beyond borders, you'll find not only destinations to explore but connections to forge, tales to unravel, and a sense of wanderlust that transcends the boundaries of nations.

Chapter 10
Sustainable Travel in Albania

As you traverse the stunning landscapes and immerse yourself in the vibrant culture of Albania, consider the profound impact your journey can have on the environment, local communities, and the preservation of the nation's cultural heritage. Sustainable travel is not just a concept; it's a commitment to responsible exploration that leaves a positive footprint on the places you visit. In this chapter, we delve into the principles of sustainable travel in Albania, inviting you to be a conscious traveler and embrace practices that ensure the beauty and authenticity of this Balkan gem endure for generations to come.

Embracing Responsible Tourism: A Pact with the Environment

Albania's natural wonders, from the rugged Accursed Mountains to the pristine beaches of the Riviera, are treasures that deserve our utmost care. As you embark on outdoor adventures and explore the national parks, adopt a leave-no-trace philosophy. Respect the trails, adhere to designated paths, and refrain from leaving any litter behind. The mountains, rivers, and coastlines of Albania are not just backdrops for your journey; they are ecosystems that thrive when treated with consideration.

Engage in eco-friendly activities that allow you to connect with nature without harming the environment. Opt for sustainable hiking, cycling, and water-based excursions that prioritize low-impact exploration. When venturing into the outdoors, support local outfitters and guides who champion environmentally conscious practices and prioritize the preservation of Albania's natural beauty.

Cultural Respect and Community Engagement

Albania's rich cultural heritage, shaped by a tapestry of influences, is a testament to the resilience and diversity of its people. As a traveler, approach cultural encounters with respect and an open mind. Engage with local communities in a meaningful way, fostering genuine connections and understanding. Be curious about the traditions, customs, and stories that define each region, and recognize the importance of cultural preservation.

Support local artisans, craftsmen, and traditional markets, where authentic products reflect the unique identity of each community. By purchasing handmade goods, you contribute to the livelihoods of local residents and help sustain traditional craftsmanship. Take the time to learn about the cultural significance of local products, from handmade textiles to traditional musical instruments, and carry a piece of Albania's heritage with you.

Participate in community-based tourism initiatives that empower local residents and promote sustainable development. Explore agrotourism farms, where you can experience rural life, savor farm-to-table cuisine, and engage in hands-on activities. By supporting community-based tourism, you become a catalyst for positive change, fostering economic opportunities that benefit local populations.

Conserving Historical Treasures

Albania's historical sites, from ancient ruins to Ottoman-era architecture, are windows into the nation's past. Treat these sites with the reverence they deserve, recognizing their cultural and historical significance. Follow established guidelines and regulations when visiting archaeological sites and monuments, and refrain from engaging in activities that may compromise their integrity.

Opt for guided tours led by knowledgeable locals or certified guides who can provide insights into the historical context of each site. Your understanding of the history and cultural significance of these places enhances the travel experience and promotes the preservation of Albania's heritage.

Contribute to the preservation efforts by supporting organizations and initiatives dedicated to the restoration and conservation of historical sites. Your awareness and engagement in these initiatives ensure that future generations can also marvel at the ancient wonders that grace the Albanian landscape.

Mindful Accommodations and Responsible Dining

Choosing sustainable accommodation is a pivotal aspect of responsible travel. Opt for hotels, guesthouses, or eco-friendly lodges that adhere to environmental best practices. Look for certifications such as Green Key or other sustainability awards, indicating a commitment to minimizing the environmental impact of the establishment.

Engage in responsible dining by sampling local, seasonal cuisine that showcases Albania's rich gastronomic heritage. Choose restaurants and eateries that prioritize the use of locally sourced ingredients, supporting farmers and promoting sustainable agricultural practices. Be mindful of your food waste and choose establishments that implement eco-friendly practices in their operations.

Reducing Your Carbon Footprint

Albania's diverse landscapes invite exploration, and your choice of transportation can significantly impact the environment. Opt for eco-friendly modes of transportation, such as public buses or shared shuttles, to minimize your carbon footprint. Consider exploring cities on foot or using bicycles, embracing a slower pace that allows you to savor the local atmosphere.

If your journey involves longer distances, explore the possibility of using trains or carpooling options. Albania's rail network connects major cities, providing a scenic and sustainable way to traverse the country. Carpooling not only reduces carbon emissions but also offers the opportunity to connect with fellow travelers and share experiences.

Consider offsetting your carbon footprint by supporting environmental initiatives or participating in community-based projects dedicated to reforestation or sustainable energy. By taking proactive measures to offset the environmental impact of your travel, you contribute to the conservation of Albania's natural beauty.

Supporting Sustainable Tourism Initiatives

Throughout Albania, various organizations and initiatives are dedicated to promoting sustainable tourism practices. Support and engage with these initiatives, whether they focus on environmental conservation, cultural preservation, or community development. Your participation contributes to the growth of responsible tourism in Albania and encourages others to follow suit.

Embrace the principles of sustainable travel not just as a checklist but as a philosophy that shapes your entire journey. By doing so, you become an advocate for the preservation of Albania's natural wonders, a guardian of its cultural heritage, and a catalyst for positive change within the communities you visit.

Closing Thoughts: A Commitment to Albania's Future

As you conclude your journey through Albania, let your footsteps echo the principles of sustainable travel. Leave behind not just memories but a legacy of responsible exploration. In doing so, you become part of a collective effort to ensure that future generations can also revel in the beauty, diversity, and authenticity that define this captivating Balkan nation.

Albania's landscapes, cultures, and histories are not static; they are dynamic narratives that evolve with each traveler's interaction. By adopting sustainable travel practices, you contribute to a positive chapter in Albania's story—one that celebrates the harmony between humans and nature, fosters cultural understanding, and leaves a lasting legacy for the generations that will follow in your footsteps.

So, fellow traveler, let sustainability guide your explorations in Albania. Immerse yourself in the wonders of this Balkan gem with a conscious heart and a commitment to leaving behind a legacy of responsible travel. Albania's landscapes and communities await your respectful embrace, and by treading lightly, you become a steward of the beauty that makes this nation an unparalleled destination for mindful adventurers. Safe travels, and may your journey in Albania be as enriching for the country as it is for you.

Conclusion
A Tapestry of Memories - Farewell to Albania

As you reach the final pages of this travel guide, I hope the words within have woven a vivid tapestry of discovery, adventure, and cultural richness—a tapestry that now resides in your memories, forever linked to the enchanting landscapes and warm-hearted people of Albania. This journey has been more than a mere exploration of a Balkan nation; it's been an odyssey through time, culture, and the breathtaking corners of a country that beckons with authenticity and allure.

Reflecting on the Journey

Think back to the moment you first set foot in Albania—the anticipation, the curiosity, and the open road stretching ahead like an unwritten chapter. Whether you arrived in bustling Tirana, ventured into the ancient ruins of Butrint, or embraced the tranquility of Theth's mountain valleys, each step has been a revelation, a brushstroke adding depth to your portrait of Albania.

Albania's allure lies in its diversity. From the bustling energy of the capital to the serene landscapes of national parks, from the timeless echoes of ancient ruins to the vibrant pulse of local markets, every experience has contributed to the multifaceted mosaic of this Balkan gem. The kaleidoscope of landscapes—mountain peaks, coastal wonders, and historical treasures—reveals a country that defies expectations and invites exploration.

Connecting with the People

One of the enduring charms of Albania is the genuine warmth of its people. From the lively conversations in cafés to the hospitality of guesthouses in remote villages, the spirit of Albania resides not just in its landscapes but in the hearts and stories of its residents. Every interaction, whether a shared meal, a welcoming smile, or a conversation with a local artisan, has added a personal touch to your journey.

Albania's cultural richness is mirrored in the diversity of its communities. The harmonious coexistence of different traditions, religions, and ethnicities is a testament to the nation's resilience and its journey toward unity. As you traveled through ancient cities, engaged with artisans, and participated in local festivals, you became part of this living tapestry, a thread connecting the past with the present.

Embracing the Spirit of Adventure

Albania, with its rugged landscapes and untamed wilderness, is a playground for adventurers. Whether you conquered the peaks of the Accursed Mountains, explored the hidden gems of the Riviera, or embarked on outdoor escapades that embraced both mountains and seas, the spirit of adventure has been your constant companion.

The outdoor wonders of Albania are not just backdrops for adrenaline-fueled activities; they are gateways to self-discovery, moments of solitude, and a communion with nature. The mountains, the rivers, and the coastlines have become more than geographical features; they are chapters in your personal adventure story—a story written with each step, each paddle, and each ascent.

Culinary Delights and Cultural Traditions

The culinary journey through Albania has been a feast for the senses, a fusion of flavors that reflects the nation's gastronomic heritage. From the hearty dishes of mountain villages to the seafood delights of coastal towns, each meal has been a celebration of local produce, traditional recipes, and the joy of shared dining experiences.

Albania's culinary delights are more than sustenance; they are expressions of cultural identity. As you savored the distinct flavors of qebapa, tasted the sweetness of baklava, or shared a cup of Turkish coffee, you immersed yourself in the traditions that have shaped Albanian cuisine for centuries. The culinary tapestry of Albania is one woven with care, passion, and a commitment to preserving the authenticity of local flavors.

Festivals and Traditions: A Living Tapestry

The festivals and traditions of Albania have been a living tapestry, weaving together the threads of history, spirituality, and community. Whether you witnessed the vibrant colors of national celebrations, the rhythmic dance of traditional music, or the serene atmosphere of religious pilgrimages, each festival offered a unique window into the soul of Albania.

As you traversed the country, from ancient cities to mountain villages, the festivals became more than cultural events; they became living connections to the people and their stories. Engaging with locals, participating in celebrations, and allowing the spirit of Albania's festivals to linger in your memories, you discovered that the country's cultural heritage is not confined to the pages of history; it's a dynamic, living tapestry that invites you to become part of the story.

Beyond Borders: Exploring Kosovo and Montenegro

Venturing beyond Albania's borders opened new chapters in your travel narrative. In Kosovo, you explored a land with a complex history, where resilience and determination shaped a vibrant present. The ancient sites of Prishtina and Peja, the rugged beauty of Rugova Gorge, and the cultural richness of Gjakova and Prizren unfolded before you, each revealing a facet of Kosovo's identity.

Crossing into Montenegro, the Bay of Kotor and the coastal towns of Kotor, Budva, and Bar invited you to bask in the Mediterranean allure. The dramatic landscapes of Durmitor National Park, the historical echoes of Cetinje, and the serpentine road along the Bay of Kotor painted a portrait of Montenegro's diversity. Beyond borders, you discovered that the Balkans are a mosaic of histories, traditions, and landscapes that invite exploration, connection, and understanding.

Sustainable Travel: Leaving a Positive Legacy

Your journey through Albania has not just been about exploration; it's been an opportunity to embrace sustainable travel practices and leave a positive legacy. From responsible outdoor adventures to cultural engagement, your choices have contributed to the preservation of the environment, the well-being of local communities, and the conservation of cultural heritage.

Albania's landscapes and cultural treasures are not just destinations; they are legacies to be safeguarded. By adopting sustainable travel practices, you have become a steward of this nation's natural and cultural heritage. Your journey is more than a collection of moments; it's a commitment to ensuring that the beauty and authenticity of Albania endure for generations to come.

A Fond Farewell

As you bid farewell to Albania, carry with you the tapestry of memories woven during your travels. The rugged peaks, the azure coastlines, the ancient ruins, and the warm smiles of the people—all are part of a collective story that now intertwines with your own. Albania, with its open arms and captivating landscapes, will forever hold a place in your heart.

May the experiences, friendships, and insights gained in Albania be a source of inspiration for future adventures. Whether you return to explore more hidden gems, reconnect with the friends you made, or share your stories with fellow travelers, know that Albania will welcome you back with the same warmth and hospitality.

In the spirit of exploration and cultural connection, may your travels continue to be a journey of discovery, understanding, and appreciation for the diverse tapestry of our world. Albania, with its untamed beauty and rich heritage, has been a remarkable chapter in your travel story. As you turn the page to new horizons, may the memories of Albania's landscapes and people remain vivid—a tapestry that accompanies you on every step of your journey.

Safe travels, fellow adventurer, and may the spirit of Albania's beauty linger in your heart wherever your wanderlust leads you.

Appendix A
Resources and Useful Information

As you embark on your journey through Albania, this appendix provides a comprehensive list of resources and practical information to enhance your travel experience. From essential contacts to helpful websites, this compilation aims to be your go-to reference for navigating the landscapes, culture, and logistics of this Balkan gem.

Embassies and Consulates:

In case of emergencies, it's essential to have the contact information for your country's embassy or consulate in Albania. Here are the embassies of some common visitor countries:

- **United States:**
    - U.S. Embassy in Tirana

Address: Rruga e Elbasanit, 103, Tirana, Albania Emergency Phone: +355 4 224 7285 Website: U.S. Embassy in Albania[1]

- **United Kingdom:**
    - British Embassy in Tirana Address: Rruga Skënderbej 12, 1000 Tirana, Albania Emergency Phone: +355 4 223 4973 Website: UK in Albania[2]
- **Canada:**
    - Embassy of Canada to Albania Address: Rr. Skënderbej, No. 13, Tirana, Albania Emergency Phone: +355 4 225 7273 Website: Embassy of Canada in Albania[3]
- **Australia:**

---

1. https://al.usembassy.gov/
2. https://www.gov.uk/world/organisations/british-embassy-tirana
3. https://www.canadainternational.gc.ca/albania-albanie/index.aspx?lang=eng

DISCOVERING ALBANIA 51

- Australian Embassy in Greece (responsible for Albania) Address: Level 2, 90 Bourke Street, Athens 10563, Greece Emergency Phone: +30 210 870 4000 Website: Australian Embassy in Greece[4]

Local Emergency Services:
In case of emergencies or immediate assistance, contact local emergency services:

- **Emergency Number (Police, Fire, Ambulance):** 112

Tourist Information Centers:
Tourist information centers can provide valuable assistance, maps, and information about local attractions. Look for these centers in major cities and tourist hubs:

- **Tirana Tourist Information Center:**
    - Location: Skanderbeg Square, Tirana, Albania
    - Contact: +355 4 222 6703
    - Website: Visit Tirana[5]
- **Gjirokastër Tourist Information Center:**
    - Location: Zekate House, Gjirokastër, Albania
    - Contact: +355 84 264 999
- **Saranda Tourist Information Center:**
    - Location: Butrinti Road, Saranda, Albania
    - Contact: +355 69 206 0490

Useful Websites:

- **Visit Albania Official Tourism Portal:**
    - Visit Albania[6]

---
4. https://greece.embassy.gov.au/
5. https://www.tirana.al/

- **Albanian National Tourism Agency:**
  - Albanian National Tourism Agency[7]
- **Albanian Riviera Tourism:**
  - Albanian Riviera[8]
- **Albanian Railway Official Website:**
  - Hekurudha Shqiptare[9]
- **Bus Services in Albania:**
  - Tirana International Bus Station[10]

Health and Safety:

- **Emergency Medical Assistance:**
  - In case of medical emergencies, dial 127.
- **Travel Insurance:**
  - Ensure you have comprehensive travel insurance that covers medical emergencies and other unforeseen circumstances.
- **Vaccinations:**
  - Check with your healthcare provider for recommended vaccinations before traveling to Albania.

Currency and Banking:

- **Currency:**
  - The official currency is the Albanian lek (ALL).
- **ATMs:**

---

6. https://www.albania.al/

7. https://albania.al/

8. https://albaniariviera.info/

9. http://www.hsh.com.al/

10. https://tiranatransport.al/

DISCOVERING ALBANIA

- ATMs are widely available in major cities. Notify your bank of your travel dates to avoid any issues with using your credit/debit cards.

Language:

- **Official Language:**
    - The official language is Albanian. English is increasingly spoken in tourist areas.

Weather:

- **Climate:**
    - Albania has a Mediterranean climate, with hot summers and mild winters. Check the weather forecast before traveling.

Transportation:

- **Driving in Albania:**
    - If you plan to drive, familiarize yourself with local traffic rules. The roads may vary in quality, so exercise caution, especially in rural areas.
- **Public Transportation:**
    - Buses and minibusses connect major cities. Check the schedule and routes in advance.
- **Rail Travel:**
    - The rail network connects major cities. Check the schedule and ticket information on the Albanian Railways[11] website.

Cultural Etiquette:

- **Greetings:**

---

11. http://www.hsh.com.al/

- A handshake is a common greeting. Use titles and last names when addressing people.
- **Dress Modestly:**
  - When visiting religious sites, dress modestly.
- **Photography:**
  - Ask for permission before taking photos of individuals, especially in rural areas.

Time Zone:

- **Time Zone:**
  - Albania is in the Central European Time (CET) zone.

Internet and Communication:

- **Internet Access:**
  - Wi-Fi is available in hotels, restaurants, and cafes in urban areas.
- **Mobile Phones:**
  - Ensure your phone is unlocked to use local SIM cards for affordable local calls and data.

Electricity:

- **Voltage:**
  - The standard voltage is 230V, and the frequency is 50Hz. The power plugs and sockets are of type C and F. Ensure you have the appropriate adapters.

Before You Go:

- **Check Visa Requirements:**
  - Verify if you need a visa before traveling to Albania. Check the

official website[12] for visa information.
- **Pack Accordingly:**
    - Pack suitable clothing for the weather and activities you plan to undertake. Don't forget essentials like travel adapters and a universal charger.

Acknowledgments:

This travel guide has been crafted with the intent to provide you with a comprehensive resource for your journey through Albania. However, please note that information may change, and it's advisable to double-check details before your trip.

Safe travels, and may your time in Albania be filled with unforgettable experiences, cultural discoveries, and the joy of exploration!

---

12. https://www.punetejashtme.gov.al/en/services/visas

Appendix B
Checklist for Long-Term Success

Use this checklist to ensure that you've covered all the essential aspects for a successful and sustainable long-term journey. Tick the boxes as you complete each item:

- ☐ **Travel Insurance:**
    - ☐ Purchased comprehensive travel insurance that covers medical emergencies, trip cancellations, and other unforeseen events.
- ☐ **Health Preparations:**
    - ☐ Checked with healthcare provider for recommended vaccinations.
    - ☐ Packed necessary prescription medications and a basic first aid kit.
- ☐ **Financial Preparedness:**
    - ☐ Informed your bank of travel dates to avoid issues with credit/debit card usage.
    - ☐ Notified credit card companies about international transactions.
- ☐ **Documentation:**
    - ☐ Checked passport expiration date (ensure it's valid for the entire duration of your stay).
    - ☐ Made photocopies of important documents (passport, insurance, tickets) and stored them

separately.

- ☐ **Communication:**
    - ☐ Unlocked your phone for international SIM card use.
    - ☐ Set up a communication plan with family and friends (share your itinerary, emergency contacts).
- ☐ **Cultural Awareness:**
    - ☐ Researched cultural norms and customs of the destination.
    - ☐ Packed appropriate clothing for cultural sites and local expectations.
- ☐ **Language:**
    - ☐ Learned basic phrases in the local language.
    - ☐ Downloaded language translation apps for assistance.
- ☐ **Accommodation:**
    - ☐ Confirmed reservations for the initial part of your journey.
    - ☐ Researched and planned long-term accommodation options.
- ☐ **Transportation:**
    - ☐ Checked transportation options within the destination (public transit, car rentals).
    - ☐ Familiarized yourself with local traffic rules if planning to drive.

- ☐ **Work/Study Arrangements:**
    - ☐ Confirmed remote work/study arrangements, if applicable.
    - ☐ Set up a dedicated workspace for productivity.
- ☐ **Finances:**
    - ☐ Set a budget for daily expenses.
    - ☐ Notified your bank of your travel destination to avoid any issues with transactions.
- ☐ **Safety and Security:**
    - ☐ Researched safe areas and potential risks in the destination.
    - ☐ Registered with your embassy or consulate if staying long-term.
- ☐ **Networking and Social Connections:**
    - ☐ Joined local expat groups or forums for networking.
    - ☐ Identified social activities or events to meet new people.
- ☐ **Local Services:**
    - ☐ Located essential services such as healthcare facilities, grocery stores, and pharmacies.
- ☐ **Adaptation:**
    - ☐ Embraced a flexible mindset for adapting to local customs and unexpected changes.
    - ☐ Opened yourself to new experiences and local

interactions.

- ☐ **Sustainable Practices:**
    - ☐ Adopted eco-friendly habits (reduce plastic use, conserve energy, support local sustainable initiatives).
- ☐ **Regular Check-ins:**
    - ☐ Scheduled regular check-ins with loved ones for updates on your well-being.
    - ☐ Monitored your mental and emotional health during the journey.
- ☐ **Cultural Immersion:**
    - ☐ Participated in local cultural activities and events.
    - ☐ Engaged with the community to foster meaningful connections.
- ☐ **Learning Opportunities:**
    - ☐ Enrolled in language courses or cultural workshops.
    - ☐ Explored opportunities for personal and professional development.
- ☐ **Reflection and Adjustment:**
    - ☐ Periodically reflected on your experiences and adjusted plans accordingly.
    - ☐ Remained open to spontaneity and unexpected opportunities.

Congratulations on Completing Your Checklist!

By completing this checklist, you've taken essential steps toward ensuring a successful and fulfilling long-term journey. May your adventure be filled with enriching experiences, personal growth, and a deeper connection to the world around you. Safe travels!

www.ingramcontent.com/pod-product-compliance
Lightning Source LLC
LaVergne TN
LVHW091552070125
800737LV00006B/113